Editors
Polly Hoffman
Gisela Lee

Editorial Manager
Karen J. Goldfluss, M.S. Ed.

Editor-in-Chief
Sharon Coan, M.S. Ed.

Cover Artist
Jessica Orlando

Art Coordinator
Denice Adorno

Creative Director
Elayne Roberts

Imaging
James Edward Grace

Product Manager
Phil Garcia

Acknowledgements
Microsoft® Excel software is
©2000 Microsoft Corporation.
All rights reserved. *Microsoft®
Excel* is a trademark of
Microsoft Corporation,
registered in U.S. and other
countries.

Publisher
Mary D. Smith, M.S. Ed.

How to Calculate Measurements

Grades 5–6

P9-ARW-527

Author

Robert Smith

Teacher Created Resources

Teacher Created Resources, Inc.
6421 Industry Way
Westminster, CA 92683
www.teachercreated.com

ISBN 13: 978-1-57690-953-9

©2000 Teacher Created Resources, Inc.
Reprinted, 2007
Made in U.S.A.

•••••••••••••••••••• Table of Contents

A Note to Teachers and Parents

Welcome to the "How to" math series! You have chosen one of over two dozen books designed to give your children the information and practice they need to acquire important concepts in specific areas of math. The goal of the "How to" math books is to give children an extra boost as they work toward mastery of the math skills established by the National Council of Teachers of Mathematics (NCTM) and outlined in grade-level scope and sequence guidelines. The NCTM standards encourage children to learn basic math concepts and skills and apply them to new situations and to real-world events. The children learn to justify their solutions through the use of pictures, numbers, words, graphs, and diagrams.

The design of this book is intended to allow it to be used by teachers or parents for a variety of purposes and needs. Each of the units contains one or more "How to" pages and two or more practice pages. The "How to" section of each unit precedes the practice pages and provides needed information such as a concept or math rule review, important terms and formulas to remember, or step-by-step guidelines necessary for using the practice pages. While most "How to" pages are written for direct use by the children, in some lower-grade level books, these pages are presented as instructional pages or direct lessons to be used by a teacher or parent prior to introducing the practice pages. In this book, each "How to" page details the concepts that will be covered in the pages that follow as well as how to teach the concepts. Many of the "How to" pages also include learning tips and extension ideas. The practice pages review and introduce new skills and provide opportunities for the children to apply the newly acquired skills. Each unit is sequential and builds upon the ideas covered in the previous unit(s).

About This Book

How to Calculate Measurements: Grades 5–6 presents a comprehensive overview of measurement for students at this level. It can be used to introduce and teach measurement to students with only minimal experience and background in this area of math.

The units in this book can be used in whole-class directed teaching instruction with the teacher or by a parent assisting his or her child through the book. This book also lends itself to use by a small group doing remedial or review work with measurement or for individuals and small groups in earlier grades engaged in enrichment or accelerated work. A teacher may want to have two tracks within his or her class with one moving at a faster pace and the other at a gradual pace appropriate to the ability or background of his or her students. The book can also be readily used in a learning center containing materials needed for each unit of instruction.

Children should be allowed to use the calculator to check computations. Other materials needed for this book include the following: ruler, yardstick, meterstick, thermometers (Fahrenheit and Celsius, preferably), and protractor. A scale, an equal-arm balance, one-ounce cups, eyedroppers, and larger liquid measuring devices would be useful. Encourage students to use manipulatives to reinforce the concepts introduced in this book. Children should practice measuring and weighing objects whenever possible. Seize the moment and have children use a penny, other coins, crayons, or a pencil to measure the number of units around a piece of paper, the dimensions of a desk, or the length and width of a door frame. Have children hold two objects and decide which weighs more.

If students have difficulty with a specific concept or unit within this book, review the material and allow students to redo the troublesome pages. Since concept development is sequential, it is advisable not to skip units. It is preferable that children find the work easy at first and to gradually advance to the more difficult concepts.

How to Calculate Measurements: Grades 5–6 highlights the use of various measuring devices and activities and emphasizes the development of proficiency in the use of basic measurement facts and processes for doing measuring. It provides a wide variety of instructional models and explanations for the gradual and thorough development of measuring concepts and processes. The units in this book are designed to match the suggestions of the National Council for the Teachers of Mathematics (NCTM). They strongly support the learning of measurement and other processes in the context of problem solving and real-world applications. Use every opportunity to have students apply these new skills in classroom situations and at home. This will reinforce the value of the skill as well as the process.

Measurements

The study of mathematics should include measurement in many facets. This book encourages and guides the use of measuring tools and the development of the actual processes of measurement as they relate to length, capacity, weight, area, perimeter, volume, time, temperature, and angle. The text stresses understanding and using the units of measurement and making and estimating measurements. It also emphasizes practical applications for everyday living.

Problem Solving

The study of mathematics should emphasize problem solving in such a way that students can use problem-solving approaches to investigate and understand the general content of mathematics. In this book, students are encouraged to solve problems involving everyday situations and real-life applications of math skills as they relate to measurements.

Communication

This book includes numerous opportunities for students to apply diagrams, charts, and measurement tools to concrete mathematical ideas. Students can relate their everyday common language to the expression of mathematical ideas and symbols on a level appropriate to their age. They can communicate the results of their measurement experiences with each other.

Reasoning

This book helps students apply logic to their math problems and asks them to justify their answers. There is an emphasis on recognizing patterns as a way of applying the units of measurement and the processes of measurement as well as the use of models, measurement manipulatives, and charts.

Connections

Throughout the book, students are encouraged to recognize and relate various measurement concepts, processes, and patterns to each other and to other mathematical concepts. They are likewise encouraged to use measurement in science and in their daily lives.

Other Standards

The pages in this book are also well aligned with other NCTM standards. These standards stress instruction of whole number computation, estimation, and geometrical concepts through real-life applications. This book also stresses that fractions, decimals, and math patterns be taught or reinforced with real-life and hands-on applications.

Facts to Know

U.S. Customary Units

The most important measuring instrument most people use is a ruler. A ruler is 1 foot long. The foot is divided into 12 inches of equal size. Each inch ends at the long line to the right of the number. Each inch is divided into 2 half inches, 4 quarter inches, 8 eighth inches, and 16 sixteenth inches.

Study the markings on this part of a ruler that has been magnified to show you how an inch is divided.

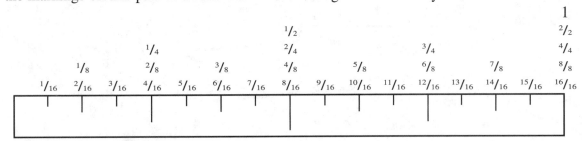

Keep these facts in mind when working with U.S. customary measurements:

- The abbreviation for foot is ft. or '.
- The abbreviation for inch is in. or ".
- A yardstick is three feet long and is divided into 36 inches.
- A yardstick is used to measure larger or longer objects. A football field is 100 yards long.
- Always start measuring from the left end of the ruler or yardstick.

Metric Units

Many rulers show both customary and metric units. The edge opposite the inch markings is divided into metric units. Metric units are often used in science. They are helpful in precisely measuring smaller objects. Because metric units are based on the number 10, it is often easier to do mathematical computations with metric measurements.

Keep these facts in mind when working with metric measurements:

- The basic unit of measure is the meter (m). A meter is slightly longer than a yard.
- A meter is evenly divided into 100 centimeters (cm).
- Each centimeter is divided into 10 millimeters (mm).

	Changing Customary to Metric	Changing Metric to Customary Length
Length	1 inch = 2.54 centimeters 1 foot = 30 centimeters 1 yard = 0.91 meters 1 mile = 1.6 kilometers	1 centimeter = 0.4 inches 1 meter = 1.09 yards 1 kilometer = 0.62 miles
Volume	1 cup = 240 milliliters 1 pint = 0.47 liters 1 quart = 0.95 liters 1 gallon = 3.79 liters	1 liter = 1.06 quarts 1 liter = 0.26 gallons
Weight	1 ounce = 28.4 grams 1 pound = 0.45 kilograms	1 gram = 0.035 ounces 1 kilogram = 2.21 pounds

1 ▶ Practice •••••••• Measuring to the Half, Quarter, Eighth, and Sixteenth of an Inch

Directions: Use a ruler and the information on page 5 to measure each of the items illustrated here to the nearest sixteenth of an inch.

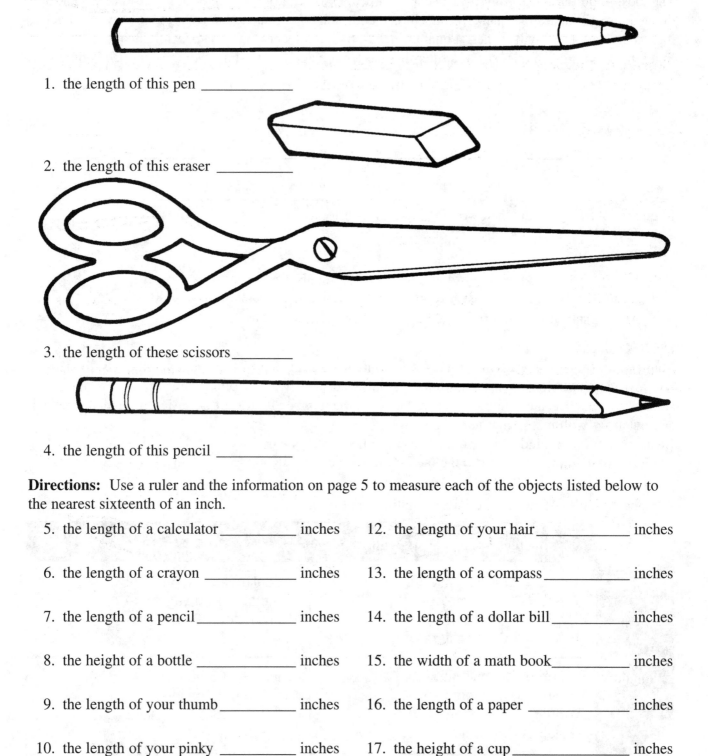

1. the length of this pen _____

2. the length of this eraser _____

3. the length of these scissors_____

4. the length of this pencil _____

Directions: Use a ruler and the information on page 5 to measure each of the objects listed below to the nearest sixteenth of an inch.

5. the length of a calculator_____ inches

6. the length of a crayon _____ inches

7. the length of a pencil_____ inches

8. the height of a bottle _____ inches

9. the length of your thumb_____ inches

10. the length of your pinky _____ inches

11. the width of a watch face _____ inches

12. the length of your hair_____ inches

13. the length of a compass_____ inches

14. the length of a dollar bill_____ inches

15. the width of a math book_____ inches

16. the length of a paper _____ inches

17. the height of a cup_____ inches

18. the length of a leaf_____ inches

This pencil is 9.5 centimeters long.

It is also 95 millimeters long.

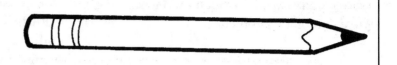

Directions: Use the metric side of a ruler to measure these objects in your classroom or home. Write the number of centimeters and millimeters for each object.

1. a piece of chalk is

    _____ cm

    _____ mm

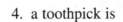

2. a paper clip is

    _____ cm

    _____ mm

3. a stapler is

    _____ cm

    _____ mm

4. a toothpick is

    _____ cm

    _____ mm

5. a nail is

    _____ cm

    _____ mm

6. a fingernail file is

    _____ cm

    _____ mm

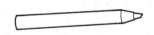

Directions: Use the metric side of a ruler to measure these objects in your classroom or home. Write the number of centimeters and millimeters for each object.

7. the length of a crayon

    _____ cm

    _____ mm

8. the length of a marker

    _____ cm

    _____ mm

9. the length of a chalkboard eraser

    _____ cm

    _____ mm

10. the length of a pencil lead

    _____ cm

    _____ mm

11. the height of a bottle

    _____ cm

    _____ mm

12. the height of a flower stem

    _____ cm

    _____ mm

13. the length of your ring (third) finger

    _____ cm

    _____ mm

14. the length of your index (first) finger

    _____ cm

    _____ mm

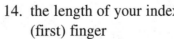

15. the width of a leaf

    _____ cm

    _____ mm

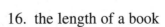

16. the length of a book

    _____ cm

    _____ mm

A yardstick is exactly 3 feet or 36 inches long.
1 yard = 3 feet = 36 inches

A meterstick is about 3 inches longer than a yardstick. A meterstick is 100 centimeters, or 1000 millimeters, long.
1 meter = 100 centimeters = 1000 millimeters

To measure objects longer than a meter or yard:

1. Place the yardstick or meterstick at one end of the object.

2. Use chalk to mark the object at the end of the stick.

3. Place the stick on the chalk line.

4. Keep a record of how many yards or meters have been measured.

5. Round the last part of the measurement to the nearest yard or meter.

Directions: Measure the following objects with a yardstick and then with a meterstick. Round your answers to the nearest yard and meter.

1. the length of a classroom _____ yd. _____ m

2. the width of a classroom _____ yd. _____ m

3. the width of a chalkboard _____ yd. _____ m

4. the length of a basketball court _____ yd. _____ m

5. your bedroom at home _____ yd. _____ m

6. the distance from your classroom to the next classroom _____ yd. _____ m

7. the length of a table in the classroom or at home _____ yd. _____ m

8. the length of a bookshelf _____ yd. _____ m

9. the length of a classroom bulletin board _____ yd. _____ m

10. the length of the longest sidewalk at school _____ yd. _____ m

11. the length of a door at home or in the classroom _____ yd. _____ m

12. the length of a school fence _____ yd. _____ m

 **How to** •••••••••••••••••••• **Compute Perimeter and Circumference**

Facts to Know

- Perimeter is the distance around all the edges of an object.
- The distance around a property such as a house, lot, or a schoolyard is the perimeter of the property.
- The following words usually indicate perimeter: border, walls, fence, edges, sides, or distance around.

Perimeters of Rectangles

The perimeter of a rectangle can be computed by any of the following ways:
- adding up all four sides of the rectangle
- adding the length and width and multiplying by 2
- using the formula: P = (l + w) x 2 or P = 2(l + w)

  (**Note:** P = perimeter, l = length, and w = width)

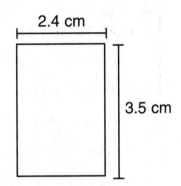

Compute the perimeter of this rectangle. The length is 3.5 centimeters and the width is 2.4 centimeters.

Add the 3.5 plus 2.4, which equals 5.9 centimeters.
Multiply by 2 to get the other two sides of the rectangle.
The total perimeter is 11.8 centimeters.

3.5 cm + 2.4 cm = 5.9 cm

5.9 cm x 2 = 11.8 cm

Perimeters of Other Polygons

Add the sides of each polygon to compute the perimeter.

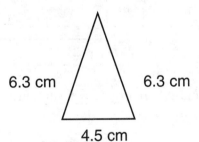

isosceles triangle
6.3 cm + 6.3 cm + 4.5 cm = 17.1 cm

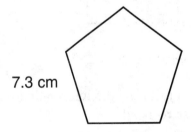

regular pentagon
7.3 cm x 5 = 36.5 cm

Circumference of a Circle

The formula for determining the circumference of a circle is 2πr or πd. (To solve, multiply 2 times r (the radius) times π (equals to approximately 3.14) or multiply d (the diameter) times 3.14.

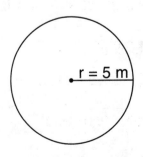

Multiply 5 times 2 times 3.14 or
5 x 2 x 3.14 = 31.4 m, so C = 31.4 meters

To compute the perimeter of a rectangle, add the length and the width and then multiply by 2.

12.5 cm + 3.3 cm = 15.8 cm

15.8 cm x 2 = 31.6 cm

P = 31.6 cm

12.5 cm

3.3 cm

Directions: Use the information on page 9 to compute the perimeters of these rectangles. Remember to label the unit of measurement—inches, feet, yards, centimeters, meters—in your answers.

1. 6.7 cm

2.4 cm

P = _____

2. 9.8 cm

3.3 cm

P = _____

3. $4\frac{1}{2}$ cm

$2\frac{1}{4}$ cm

P = _____

4. $5\frac{1}{4}$ ft.

3 ft.

P = _____

5. $5\frac{1}{8}$ in.

$2\frac{1}{2}$ in.

P = _____

6. $6\frac{1}{16}$ cm

$3\frac{1}{8}$ cm

P = _____

Directions: Use a ruler and the information on pages 5 and 9 to help you measure and compute the perimeters of these rectangles.

7. a math book cover

length _____

width _____

P = _____

8. a sheet of paper

length _____

width _____

P = _____

9. a paperback book cover

length _____

width _____

P = _____

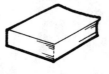

10. a desk

length _____

width _____

P = _____

To compute the perimeter of a regular polygon, in which all sides are equal, multiply the length of one side by the number of sides.

Directions: Compute the perimeter of each of the regular polygons illustrated below. Remember to label the unit of measurement—inches, feet, yards, centimeters, meters—in your answer.

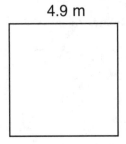

4.9 m

4.9 m x 4 = 19.6 m

1. 5.2 cm
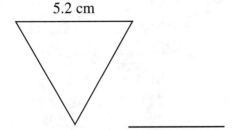

2. $2\frac{1}{4}$ in.
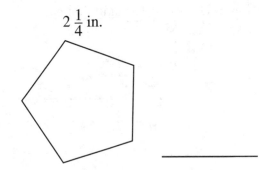

3. 6.1 m
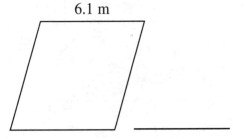

4. $3\frac{1}{8}$ ft.
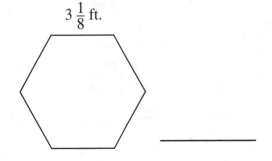

5. 9.3 m
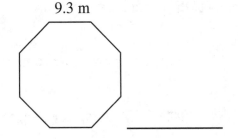

6. 8 yd.
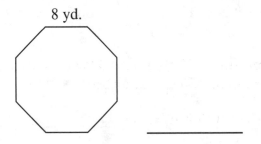

7. 22.9 cm
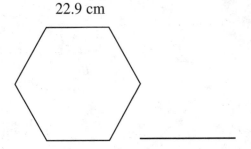

8. 11.7 m
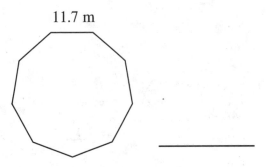

To compute the perimeter of an irregular polygon, add the lengths of the sides.

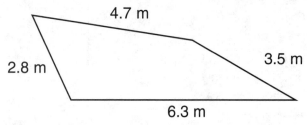

P = 4.7 m + 3.5 m + 6.3 m + 2.8 m = 17.3 m

Directions: Use the information on pages 5 and 9 to help you compute the perimeters of these polygons. Remember to label the unit of measurement—inches, feet, yards, centimeters, meters—in your answer.

1. P = _____

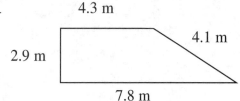

2. P = _____

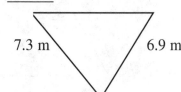

3. P = _____

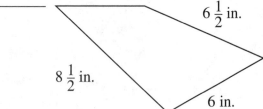

4. P = _____

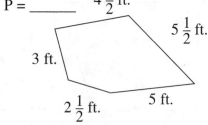

Directions: Use the information on page 9 to help you compute the circumferences of these circles. (C = 2πr or C = πd)

5.

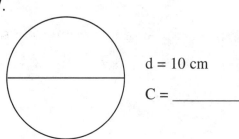

r = 4 m

C = _____

6.

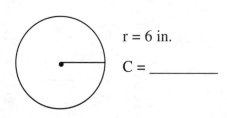

r = 6 in.

C = _____

7.

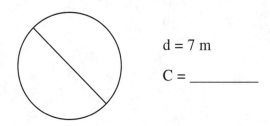

d = 10 cm

C = _____

8.

d = 7 m

C = _____

Facts to Know

Area of a Rectangle

The area of a rectangle is computed by multiplying the length times the width.

The formula is written: A = l x w (Area = length times width) or A = b x h (Area = base times height).

The answer is given in square units. They are usually abbreviated like this: 4 sq. m or 4 m².

> **Example:** This rectangle is 6 centimeters long and 2 centimeters wide.

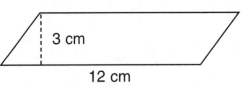

2 cm

6 cm

A = l x w

A = 2 cm x 6 cm

A = 12 cm²

Area of a Parallelogram

The area of a parallelogram is computed by multiplying the base times the height.

The formula is written: A = b x h or Area = base times height.

> **Example:** This parallelogram has a base of 12 cm and a height of 3 cm.

3 cm

12 cm

A = b x h

A = 12 cm x 3 cm

A = 36 cm²

Area of a Triangle

The area of a triangle is computed by multiplying $\frac{1}{2}$ times the base times the height.

A triangle is always one half of a rectangle or parallelogram.

The formula is written: $A = \frac{1}{2}$ (b x h) or $\frac{b \times h}{2}$

> **Example:** This triangle has a base of 10 cm and a height of 4 cm.

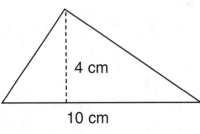

4 cm

10 cm

$A = \frac{1}{2}$ (b x h)

$A = \frac{1}{2}$ x 10 cm x 4 cm

A = 20 cm²

Area of a Circle

The area of a circle is computed by multiplying pi (which is approximately 3.14) times the radius times itself.

> **Example:** This circle has a radius of 4 cm.

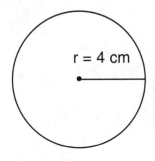

r = 4 cm

A = πr² (Area = pi x the radius x the radius)

A = 3.14 x 4 cm x 4 cm

A = 50.24 cm²

All rectangles are also parallelograms. They have two pairs of parallel sides.

The formula for the area of a rectangle is

A = l x w or A = b x h

The formula for the area of a parallelogram is **A = bh**

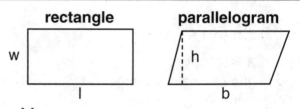

rectangle

w

l

parallelogram

h

b

Directions: Use the information on page 13 to compute the areas of these rectangles and parallelograms. Remember to indicate the unit—square feet, square meters, square inches, etc.—with the answer.

1.

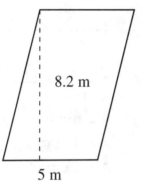

8.2 m

5 m

A = _____

2.

18 yd.

7 yd.

A = _____

3.

9 cm

7.5 cm

A = _____

4.

3.2 m

1.9 m

A = _____

6.

$3\frac{1}{4}$ in.

5 in.

A = _____

5.

$8\frac{1}{2}$ ft.

4 ft.

A = _____

8.

75 mm

100 mm

A = _____

7.

92 m

40 m

A = _____

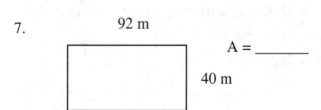

This is the formula for computing the area of a triangle:

$A = \frac{1}{2} b \times h$ (or) $A = \frac{b \times h}{2}$

$A = \frac{1}{2} \times 8 \times 4$

$A = 16 \text{ m}^2$

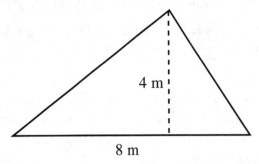

4 m

8 m

Directions: Use the information on page 13 to compute the areas of these triangles. Remember to indicate the unit—square feet, square meters, square inches, etc.—with the answer.

1. A = _____

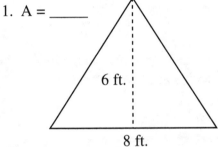

6 ft.

8 ft.

2. A = _____

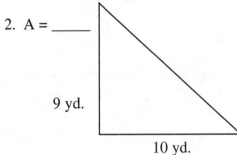

9 yd.

10 yd.

3. A = _____

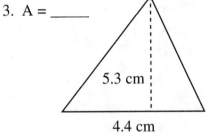

5.3 cm

4.4 cm

4. A = _____

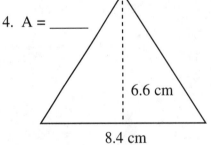

6.6 cm

8.4 cm

5. A = _____

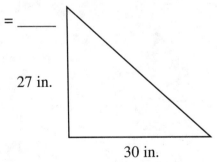

27 in.

30 in.

6. A = _____

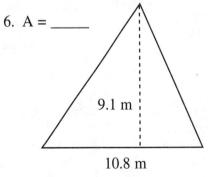

9.1 m

10.8 m

7. A = _____

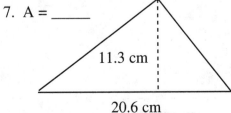

11.3 cm

20.6 cm

8. A = _____

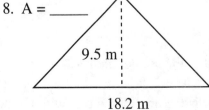

9.5 m

18.2 m

This is the formula for computing the area of a circle.

A = πr² (Area = pi x the radius x the radius)

The most efficient way to calculate the area of a circle is to multiply the radius times itself and then multiply that product times pi, which is approximately equal to 3.14.

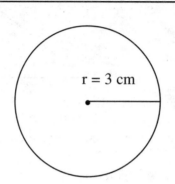

r = 3 cm

r = 3 cm

A = πr²

A = 3.14 x 3 cm x 3 cm

A = 28.26 cm²

Directions: Use the information on page 13 to compute the areas of these circles. Remember to indicate the unit—square feet, square meters, square inches, etc—with the answer.

1.

r = 4 m

A = _____

2.

r = 5 cm

A = _____

3.

r = 10 cm

A = _____

4.

r = 12 cm

A = _____

5.

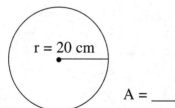

r = 20 cm

A = _____

6.

r = 14 ft.

A = _____

7. What is the area of a circle with a radius of 15 inches?_____

8. What is the area of a circle with a radius of 25 meters?_____

Facts to Know

Volume of a Rectangular Prism

To determine how much material can fit into an empty rectangular object such as a box or in any other rectangular prism:

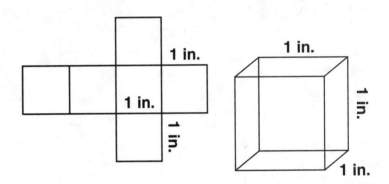

length = 4 cm

height = 2 cm

width = 3 cm

1. Measure the length, the width, and the height of the prism.

2. Multiply the length times the width times the height.

3. Record the answer in cubic units.

4. The formula is V = l x w x h or Volume = length x width x height

5. The answer is V = 4 cm x 3 cm x 2 cm = 24 cubic centmeters (or cm³)

Cubic Units

- A cubic foot is 1 foot long, 1 foot wide, and 1 foot high.

- A cubic centimeter is 1 centimeter long, 1 centimeter wide, and 1 centimeter high.

- A cubic inch is 1 inch long, 1 inch wide, and 1 inch high.

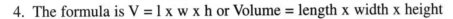

1 in.

1 in.

1 in.

1 in.

1 in.

1 in.

Volume of a Cylinder

A cylinder is a round tube with two circular, flat faces. You can compute the volume of a cylinder this way:

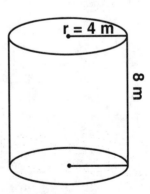

r = 4 m

8 m

1. Multiply the radius times itself and this product times pi (3.14) to compute the area of the circular face.

2. Multiply this area times the length (or height) of the cylinder.

3. The formula is V = π(r²) x h

4. The answer is V = 3.14 x (4)² x 8 = 401.92 cubic meters (or m³).

The formula for the volume of a rectangular prism is

V = l x w x h

V = 5 ft. x 3 ft. x 2 ft.

V = 30 ft.³

The answer is always expressed in cubic units.

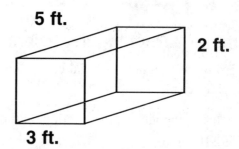

Directions: Use the information on page 17 to compute the volume of each figure represented below.

1.
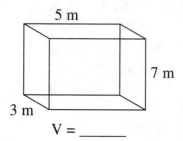
5 m
7 m
3 m
V = _____

2.
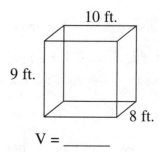
10 ft.
9 ft.
8 ft.
V = _____

3.
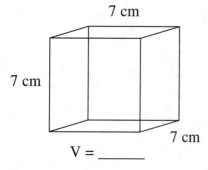
7 cm
7 cm
7 cm
V = _____

4.
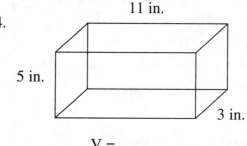
11 in.
5 in.
3 in.
V = _____

5.
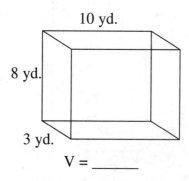
10 yd.
8 yd.
3 yd.
V = _____

6.
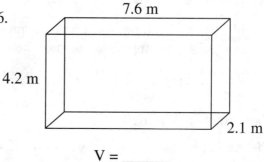
7.6 m
4.2 m
2.1 m
V = _____

7. What is the volume of a box which is 5.6 m long, 7.2 m wide, and 2.3 m high? V = _____

8. What is the volume of a prism 9.1 cm long, 10.6 cm wide, and 7.2 cm high? V = _____

9. What is the volume of a prism which is 12 feet long, 12 feet wide, and 12 feet high? V = _____

10. What is the volume of a prism $3\frac{1}{2}$ feet long, $5\frac{1}{2}$ feet wide, and $4\frac{1}{2}$ feet high? V = _____

This is the formula for computing the volume of a cylinder: $\mathbf{V = \pi r^2 \times h}$

- Multiply the radius times itself.
- Multiply that product times 3.14.
- Multiply that product times the height.
- Express the answer in cubic units.

V = πr² x h

V = 3.14 x 3 cm x 3 cm x 4 cm

V = 113.04 cm³

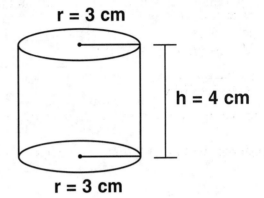

r = 3 cm

h = 4 cm

r = 3 cm

Directions: Use the information on page 17 to compute the volume of each cylinder. Remember to indicate the units—cubic feet, cubic meters, cubic inches, etc.—with the answer.

1.
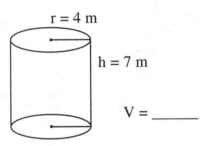
r = 4 m
h = 7 m
V = _____

4.
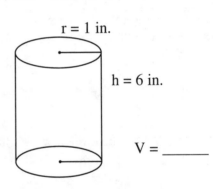
r = 1 in.
h = 6 in.
V = _____

2.
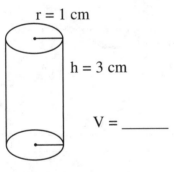
r = 1 cm
h = 3 cm
V = _____

5.
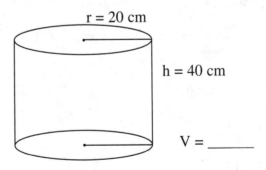
r = 20 cm
h = 40 cm
V = _____

3.
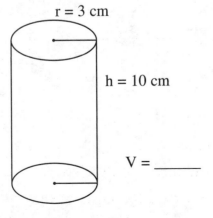
r = 3 cm
h = 10 cm
V = _____

6.
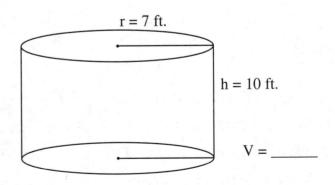
r = 7 ft.
h = 10 ft.
V = _____

Directions: Find the objects listed in the problems below in your classroom or your house. Find the length, width, and height of these objects and then calculate the volume of each object in cubic inches.

1. pencil box

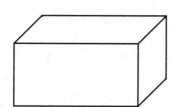

l = _____ in.

w = _____ in.

h = _____ in.

V = _____ in.³

3. tabletop

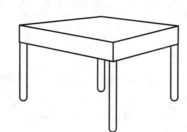

l = _____ in.

w = _____ in.

h = _____ in.

V = _____ in.³

2. storage box

l = _____ in.

w = _____ in.

h = _____ in.

V = _____ in.³

4. tissue box

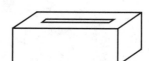

l = _____ in.

w = _____ in.

h = _____ in.

V = _____ in.³

Directions: Find the objects listed below in your classroom or home. Measure the radius and height of each object and calculate the volume.

5. soup can

h = _____ in.

r = _____ in.

V = _____ in.³

7. soda can

h = _____ in.

r = _____ in.

V = _____ in.³

6. candle

h = _____ in.

r = _____ in.

V = _____ in.³

8. hair spray can

h = _____ in.

r = _____ in.

V = _____ in.³

Facts to Know

Units of Measurement

There are some basic units of measurement for light objects.

- The gram is a metric unit. A large paper clip weighs about 1 gram. Scientists measure in grams. Most countries measure in grams.

- The ounce is a customary unit of measurement. It is equal to about 28 grams. An ounce would weigh about as much as 28 paper clips or 1 AA battery. Ounces are commonly used in daily life.

- Extremely small amounts of medicine or chemicals may be weighed in milligrams or occasionally in grams.

- Heavier objects are weighed in pounds or kilograms.

Customary Units	Metric Units
1/28 ounce = 1 gram 16 ounces = 1 pound 2000 pounds = 1 ton	1/1000 gram = 1 milligram 10 grams = 1 decagram 100 grams = 1 hectogram 1000 grams = 1 kilogram

Equal-Arm Balance

The equal-arm balance compares the weight of a standard unit of measure, such as a gram weight or an ounce weight, in one cup to the weight of an object in the other cup.

Use an equal-arm balance to determine how many grams a chalkboard eraser weighs.

1. Use large paper clips as gram weights. (Some large paper clips weigh a gram and some weigh slightly more or less than a gram, but they are close enough for this activity.)

2. Place the object to be weighed, the eraser, in one cup.

3. In the other cup put gram weights, such as large paper clips, or ounce weights, until the two cups are evenly balanced.

4. Count the paper clips or other weights as you put them in the cup.

Scale

A scale such as a postal scale indicates the weight of an object set on the tray of the scale by a series of marks to indicate ounces or pounds. (Some scales have metric markings.)

Scales are very easy to use. Place the object on the tray and read the weight to which the indicator is pointing.

Directions: Use an equal-arm balance and large paper clips to weigh these objects. Record the weight to the nearest gram. (Answers may vary.)

1. pencil _____ grams

2. crayon _____ grams

3. quarter _____ grams

4. pen _____ grams

5. 1 sheet of paper _____ grams

6. pink eraser _____ grams

7. ruler _____ grams

8. computer diskette _____ grams

9. AA battery _____ grams

10. protractor _____ grams

11. 2 dice _____ grams

12. scissors _____ grams

13. math compass _____ grams

14. small pencil sharpener _____ grams

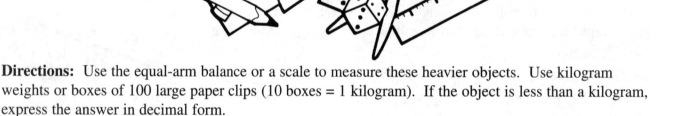

Directions: Use the equal-arm balance or a scale to measure these heavier objects. Use kilogram weights or boxes of 100 large paper clips (10 boxes = 1 kilogram). If the object is less than a kilogram, express the answer in decimal form.

15. math book _____ kilograms

16. dictionary _____ kilograms

17. can of soup _____ kilograms

18. videocassette _____ kilograms

19. encyclopedia _____ kilograms

20. bar of soap _____ kilograms

21. 2 decks of cards _____ kilograms

22. a bag of 100 marbles _____ kilograms

Directions: Use a scale, if available, or an equal-arm balance or estimate the weight of each object in ounces.

1. videocassette _____ ounces

6. box of crayons _____ ounces

2. pair of glasses _____ ounces

7. thin workbook _____ ounces

3. paperback book _____ ounces

8. pad of paper _____ ounces

4. small radio _____ ounces

9. cassette _____ ounces

5. wallet _____ ounces

10. board eraser _____ ounces

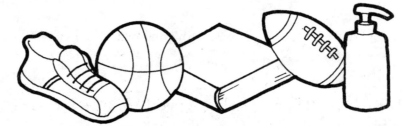

Directions: Use a scale or estimate the weights of these objects. Record your answers in pounds (lb.) and ounces (oz.).

11. dictionary _____ lb. _____ oz.

16. football _____ lb. _____ oz.

12. encyclopedia _____ lb. _____ oz.

17. stone _____ lb. _____ oz.

13. tennis shoe _____ lb. _____ oz.

18. basketball _____ lb. _____ oz.

14. large can of soup _____ lb. _____ oz.

19. six paperback books _____ lb. _____ oz.

15. bottle of liquid soap _____ lb. _____ oz.

20. textbook _____ lb. _____ oz.

Directions: Use the information on page 21 to do the following problems.

1. A ream of paper contains 500 sheets. A set of 5 sheets of paper weighs about 1 ounce. How many pounds and ounces does the ream weigh? _____ lb. _____ oz.

2. For a special art project, each child in the sixth grade needed a 25-lb. bag of clay. There were 92 sixth graders. How much clay did the teachers need? _____ tons _____ lb.

3. A videocassette weighs 1/2 pound. How many videocassettes would weigh a ton? _____

4. One kind of medicine uses 10 milligrams of medicine for each pill. How many pills would 1 gram of medicine make? _____

5. Using the above problem, how many pills would 1 kilogram of medicine make? _____

6. A paperback dictionary weighs 1 1/2 pounds. How many dictionaries would be in 1 1/2 tons? _____

7. A stapler weighs 8 ounces. How many staplers would be in a 3-ton shipment? _____

8. A science experiment called for 1 decagram of baking soda per person. How many people could do the experiment with 1 kilogram of baking soda? _____

9. One science student studies 5 milligrams of dust with a microscope. How much dust would be needed for 100 students? _____

10. It takes about 2.2 kilograms to equal 1 pound. How many kilograms would be in 100 pounds? _____

11. How many kilograms would be in 1 ton? _____

12. About how many large (1g) paper clips would it take to weigh 1 pound? _____

13. One calculator weighs 5 ounces. How many calculators would be in a 1-ton shipment? _____

14. One small camera weighs 2.5 hectograms. How many cameras would be in a 10-kilogram shipment? _____

6 ▷ How to ●●●●●●●●●●●●●●●●●●●● **Work with Liquid Measurements (Capacity)**

Facts to Know

- The most common small unit of liquid measure in daily use is the fluid ounce.

- A fluid ounce (fl. oz.) is equal to 6 teaspoons (tsp.) of liquid.

- The most basic small unit of liquid measure in the metric system is the milliliter.

- 1 fluid ounce = about 30 milliliters.

Chart of Liquid Measures

Customary Units	Metric Units
8 fluid ounces = 1 cup	100 milliliters = 1 centiliter
16 fluid ounces = 1 pint	1,000 milliliters = 1 liter
2 cups = 1 pint	10 centiliters = 1 liter
32 fluid ounces = 1 quart	1,000 liters = 1 kiloliter
2 pints = 1 quart	
4 cups = 1 quart	
128 fluid ounces = 1 gallon	
4 quarts = 1 gallon	
8 pints = 1 gallon	

Measuring Tools

- An eyedropper holds about 1 milliliter.

- It would take about 30 eyedroppers to hold 1 fluid ounce.

- A medicine cup usually holds 1 fluid ounce.

- A measuring cup usually holds either 8 or 16 fluid ounces.

Sample A

Rita wanted to make pancakes for breakfast. She had pancake mix but needed to pick up some other ingredients at the store. She bought a one-half gallon of milk and a 32-ounce container of maple syrup. What are the metric equivalents to the two ingredients that Rita bought at the store? Use milliliters or liters in your answer.

$\frac{1}{2}$ gallon of milk = 64 fluid ounces of milk

(Remember, 1 fluid ounce = 30 mL, and 1,000 milliliters = 1 liter)

64 x 30 mL = 1,920 mL = 1.92 liters

So, $\frac{1}{2}$ gallon of milk is equivalent to 1.92 liters of milk.

32 fluid ounces of maple syrup = 32 x 30 mL = 960 mL

So, 32 fluid ounces of maple syrup is equivalent to 960 mL of maple syrup.

Directions: Use the information on page 25 to help you do these problems.

1. 1 cup = _____ fluid ounces

2. 2 cups = _____ fluid ounces

3. 4 cups = _____ fluid ounces

4. 6 cups = _____ fluid ounces

5. 8 cups = _____ fluid ounces

6. 9 cups = _____ fluid ounces

7. 1 quart = _____ fluid ounces

8. 2 quarts = _____ fluid ounces

9. 5 quarts = _____ fluid ounces

10. 3 quarts = _____ fluid ounces

11. How many quarts will a 1-gallon container hold? _____

12. How many quarts are equal to 4 gallons? _____

13. How many fluid ounces are in 1 gallon? _____

14. How many quarts are in a 15-gallon tank of gas? _____

15. How many fluid ounces are in a 15-gallon tank of gasoline? _____

16. 1 pint = _____ fluid ounces

17. 3 pints = _____ fluid ounces

18. 7 pints = _____ fluid ounces

19. 5 gallons = _____ pints

20. 11 gallons = _____ cups

21. 15 gallons = _____ pints

22. 10 gallons = _____ fluid ounces

23. 17 pints = _____ cups

24. How many total fluid ounces are in 1 gallon, 1 quart, and 1 pint? _____ fl. oz.

25. How many total fluid ounces are in 2 gallons, 2 quarts, 1 pint, and 1 cup? _____ fl. oz.

| 1 fluid ounce = 30 milliliters |

Directions: Use the chart on page 25 to help you do these problems.

1. How many milliliters will fit into 1 fluid ounce? _____ mL

2. How many milliliters will a cup hold? _____ mL

3. How many milliliters will a liter hold? _____ mL

4. How many milliliters will a quart hold? _____ mL

5. How many more milliliters will a liter hold than a quart? _____ mL

6. How many milliliters will a pint hold? _____ mL

7. How many milliliters will a gallon hold? _____ mL

8. How many liters will fit in a 1-gallon container? _____ L

9. How many liters will fit in a 10-gallon container? _____ L

10. How many liters are in an 18-gallon tank of gasoline? _____ L

11. How many liters are in 1,000 quarts of milk? _____ L

12. How many liters are in 25 gallons of orange juice? _____ L

13. How many liters are in 200 pints of water? _____ L

14. How many liters are in 2,000 quarts of lemonade? _____ L

15. How many liters are in 750 pints of liquid detergent? _____ L

Directions: Use the information on page 25 to help you do the following problems.

1. A spaghetti recipe calls for 8 cups of water. How many quarts of water are needed? _____

2. A cook needed to add 3 milliliters of food coloring to each cup of water. How much food coloring would she need for a quart of water? _____

3. A scientist added 5 mL of acid to a cup of water. How much would she need for a gallon of water? _____

4. A chemistry student was adding 7 milliliters of ammonia to a cup of vinegar. Using the same formula, how much ammonia would she add to 3 gallons of vinegar? _____

5. A sixth grader found that 20 milliliters of water would sit on the head of a penny without spilling. How many penny heads could he cover with a liter of water? _____

6. A fifth grade student wanted to add 9 milliliters of dish soap to each cup of water in her 3-gallon container. How many milliliters did she add to the 3 gallons of water? _____

7. Your best friend wanted to make a soap solution by adding 3 fluid ounces of soap to each pint of water. How much soap did she add to a gallon of water? _____

8. You decided to make a soapy water solution using 12 milliliters of water to every cup of water. How many milliliters did you add to 2 gallons of water? _____

9. One of your classmates was able to place 30 milliliters of water on the head of a quarter. How many quarter heads could she cover with a gallon of water? _____

10. Your neighbor wants to give 5 gallons of water to her roses using a 1-liter watering container. How many liters will she use? _____

11. A painter's bucket will hold 10 cups of paint. How many times will he fill his bucket to use 5 gallons of paint? _____

12. A custodian uses 1.5 cups of floor cleaner for every quart of water. How many cups of cleaner will he use with 8 gallons of water? _____

Facts to Know

- A protractor is used to measure the exact size of an angle in terms of the number of degrees between 0° and 180°.

- There are usually two sets of numbers on a protractor—one set running from left to right and the other set from right to left.

- These two sets of numbers make it easier to line up the protractor on any angle, regardless of the direction of the angle.

- The halfway point of every protractor is 90°. It is only written once.

Using the Protractor

To measure an angle with a protractor do the following:

1. Place the circle at the bottom center of the protractor (or comparable vertex marker) directly on the vertex (point) of the angle.

2. Carefully line up the black line at the bottom of the protractor (or comparible baseline indicator) along the bottom ray of the angle.

3. Find the pair of numbers where the top ray of the angle intersects the degree markings on the protractor.

4. Determine whether the angle is acute, obtuse, right, or straight.

5. Decide which number fits this angle.

Angle Names and Facts

- Acute angles are less than 90°. Acute angles can face in any direction.

- Right angles are exactly 90°. Right angles can face in any direction.

- Obtuse angles are more than 90° but less than 180°. Obtuse angles can face in any direction.

- A straight angle is exactly 180°.

- A reflex angle is more than 180° and less than 360°.

acute angle   right angle

obtuse angle   straight angle

reflex angle

Using the Protractor with a Circle

To divide a circle with a protractor do the following:

1. Draw a radius from the exact center of the circle to the circumference.

2. Line up the protractor, using the radius as one of the rays of the angle.

3. Mark the number of degrees you want the angle to be.

4. Draw another radius from this mark to the center point.

 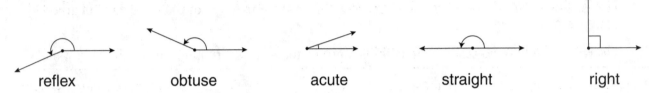

Study these types of angles.

Directions: Use the information on page 29 and your protractor to measure the number of degrees in each angle and to name the type of angle represented.

1.
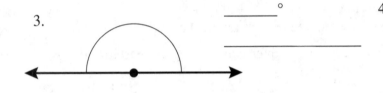

_____ °

_____

2.
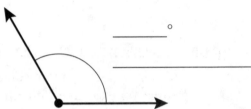

_____ °

_____

3.

_____ °

_____

4.

_____ °

_____

5.
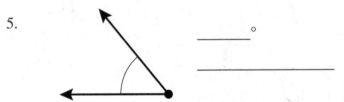

_____ °

_____

6.
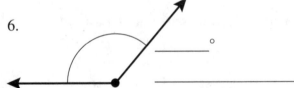

_____ °

_____

7.

_____ °

_____

8.

_____ °

_____

9.

_____ °

_____

10.

_____ °

_____

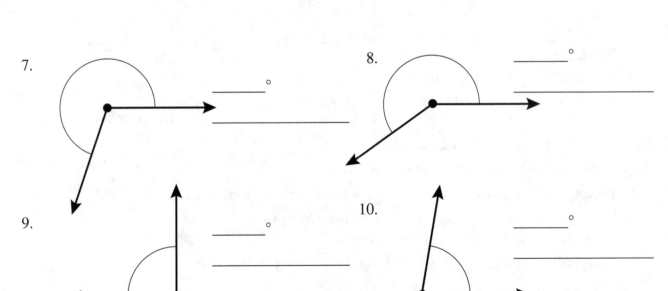

Facts to Know

- The middle letter names the location of each angle. Angle ABC is at point B. Angle CEF is at point E.

- The internal angles of a triangle should total 180°.

Directions: Use the information above and on page 29 to measure each angle in these triangles. List the degrees for each angle and the total degrees for each triangle.

1.

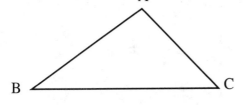

       <BAC = _____°

       <CBA = _____°

       <ACB = _____°

       △ABC = _____°

2.

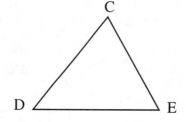

       <CDE = _____°

       <ECD = _____°

       <DEC = _____°

       △DEC = _____°

3.

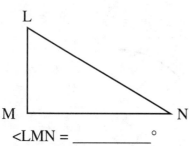

       <LMN = _____°

       <MNL = _____°

       <MLN = _____°

       △LMN = _____°

4.

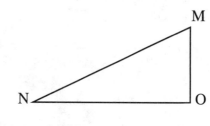

       <MNO = _____°

       <OMN = _____°

       <MON = _____°

       △MNO = _____°

5.

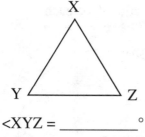

       <XYZ = _____°

       <ZXY = _____°

       <YZX = _____°

       △XYZ = _____°

6.

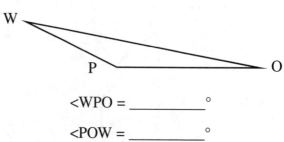

       <WPO = _____°

       <POW = _____°

       <PWO = _____°

       △WPO = _____°

Sample

A circle has 360°.

This circle has been divided into 3 sections.

Each section is 120°.

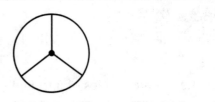

Directions: Use the information on page 29 and a protractor to divide each circle as instructed.

1. 4 sections/90° each

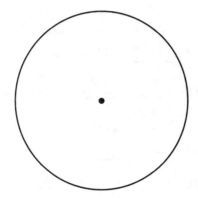

2. 6 sections/60° each

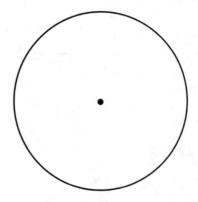

3. 8 sections/45° each

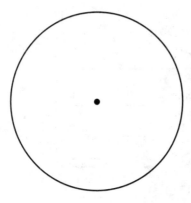

4. 3 sections/120° each

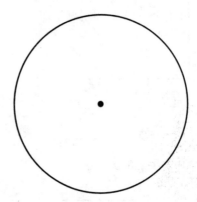

5. 9 sections/40° each

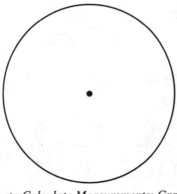

6. 12 sections/30° each

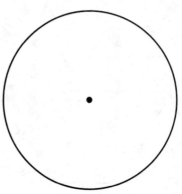

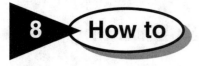

Facts to Know

Time

> A.M. = morning - 12:00 A.M. (midnight) to 11:59 A.M.
>
> P.M. = afternoon - 12:00 P.M. (noon) to 11:59 P.M.
>
> 60 seconds = 1 minute
>
> 60 minutes = 1 hour
>
> 24 hours = 1 day

To compute elapsed time within the morning or within the afternoon, subtract the smaller number from the larger number. Remember to regroup (borrow) with 60 minutes.

Sample

Because you cannot subtract 0 minutes from 38 minutes, subtract 1 hour from the 9:00 P.M. and convert it to 60 minutes. So when you calculate how much time elapsed between 9:00 P.M. and 7:38 p.m., the final answer is 1 hour 22 minutes.

$$\begin{array}{r} 8{:}60 \\ \cancel{9{:}00} \text{ P.M.} \\ -\ 7{:}38 \text{ P.M.} \\ \hline 1{:}22 \text{ (1 hr 22 min)} \end{array}$$

To add elapsed time, add the two measurements of time together.

Sample

When you add the two measurements of time together, you have an answer of 218 days 49 hrs 60 min, but you know that you convert some of the minutes to hours and some hours into days. Using the chart at the top of the page, you know that 24 hours = 1 day so 49 hours = 2 days 1 hour. Similarly, you know that 60 minutes = 1 hour so after you made all the conversions, the final answer is 220 days and 2 hours have elapsed.

$$\begin{array}{l} 206 \text{ days} \quad 2 \text{ hrs} \quad 5 \text{ min} \\ +\ 12 \text{ days} \quad 47 \text{ hrs} \quad 55 \text{ min} \\ \hline 218 \text{ days} \quad 49 \text{ hrs} \quad 60 \text{ min} = 220 \text{ days} \quad 2 \text{ hrs} \end{array}$$

Calendar Facts

	28-Day Month	31-Day Months
7 days = 1 week	February (29 days in leap year)	January
52 weeks = 1 year		March
10 years = 1 decade		May
10 decades = 1 century	**30-Day Months**	July
10 centuries = 1 millennium	September	August
	April	October
	June	December
	November	

- Time from the approximate date of the birth of Christ until the present moves progressively from 1 to 2000 +. It is called A.D. (anno domini—in the year of our Lord).

- Time before the birth of Christ counts back from 1 to the earliest recorded history, about 5,000 years. It is called B.C. (before Christ) or B.C.E. ("before the common era").

- To compute the passage of years within B.C. or within A.D., subtract the lower number from the higher number.

- To compute the passage of years from B.C. to A.D., add the B.C. date to the A.D. date.

Directions: Using the information on page 33, compute the elapsed time for the problems below. Remember to regroup when needed.

1. 11:35 A.M.
    − 8:00 A.M.

2. 11:10 A.M.
    − 9:30 A.M.

3. 10:25 P.M.
    − 4:00 P.M.

4. 9:25 P.M.
    − 2:30 P.M.

5. 9:55 A.M.
    − 7:20 A.M.

6. 11:02 A.M.
    − 2:56 A.M.

7. 9:05 P.M.
    − 1:09 P.M.

8. 6:15 P.M.
    − 3:59 P.M.

9. 134 days 4 hrs 23 min
    + 56 days 9 hrs   9 min

10. 67 days 19 hrs 15 min
    + 23 days   8 hrs 24 min

11. 12 wks 20 days 14 hrs 41 min
    + 19 wks   3 days 23 hrs 59 min

12. 39 wks 15 days 13 hrs 59 min
    − 25 wks   2 days   8 hrs 53 min

13. 40 days   3 hrs 50 min
    − 13 days 15 hrs 16 min

14. 75 days 23 hrs 15 min
    − 62 days   3 hrs 50 min

February

S	M	T	W	T	F	S
		1	2	3	4	5
6	7	8	9	10	11	12
13	14	15	16	17	18	19
20	21	22	23	24	25	26
27	28	29				

March

S	M	T	W	T	F	S
			1	2	3	4
5	6	7	8	9	10	11
12	13	14	15	16	17	18
19	20	21	22	23	24	25
26	27	28	29	30	31	

Directions: Study the two calendars above which are for consecutive months. Use the information on page 33 to help you answer the following questions.

1. Which two months of the year are shown above? _____ _____

2. How do you know which months are shown?_____

3. What is the date exactly 2 weeks after February 5th?_____

4. What is the date exactly 6 weeks after February 22nd? _____

5. What is the date exactly 5 weeks after Lincoln's Birthday (February 12th)?_____

6. How many Fridays are in March? _____

7. How many days were in the month before the first calendar? _____

8. How many days are left in the year after the second calendar? _____

9. What date is the 61st day of the year on this calendar? _____

10. What date is the 360th day of this year?_____

11. Easter was the fourth Sunday of April on the calendar year shown above.

    What was the date? _____

12. What day of the week is May 1?_____

This is a time line of important math inventions and discoveries.

B.C.   **A.D.**

c. 2000 B.C.

The Babylonians developed a form of place value based on the number 60.

c. 1800 B.C.

The Babylonians developed a multiplication table.

c. 1700 B.C.

The Sumerians discovered squares and square roots and a value for pi.

c. 1350 B.C.

The Chinese developed decimals.

c. 1000 B.C.

The Chinese developed a primitive abacus.

c. 300 B.C.

Euclid, a Greek mathematician, wrote a textbook on geometry and the theory of numbers.

c. 100 B.C.

Chinese mathematicians used negative numbers.

876 A.D.
The symbol for zero was used in India.

1202 A.D.
Arabic numerals were introduced in Europe.

1492 A.D.
The decimal point was first used.

1514 A.D.
Plus and minus signs were used in equations.

1525 A.D.
The symbol for square roots ($\sqrt{}$) was first used.

1617 A.D.
John Napier invented Napier's Bones, an efficient calculating device.

c. 1622 A.D.
The slide rule was invented to improve speed in calculations.

1631 A.D.
The multiplication sign (x) was first used.

1637 A.D.
Descartes developed the coordinate system.

1642 A.D.
Blaise Pascal invented an adding machine.

1666 A.D.
Isaac Newton developed calculus.

1813 A.D.
The tangram first appeared in print.

1946 A.D.
The first digital computer, ENIAC, was invented.

Directions: Use the information on page 33 and this time line to do these computations. Use the date of the current year to calculate the solutions to these problems.

1. How many years ago was the slide rule invented?

   _____

2. How many years ago did the Babylonians develop a multiplication table?

   _____

3. How many years ago was the multiplication sign first used? _____

4. How many years ago did the tangram first appear in print?_____

5. How many years ago did the Chinese develop the abacus? _____

6. How many years ago did the Chinese begin to use negative numbers? _____

7. How many years ago did Napier's Bones get invented?_____

8. How many years ago did Newton develop calculus? _____

Facts to Know

- The temperature on a thermometer is determined by finding the level of the red mercury in the tube and the number on the temperature scale across from it.
- The temperature is written in numbers with the ° sign. For example, 80° F is read: 80 degrees Fahrenheit.

Fahrenheit

- The Fahrenheit scale records the freezing point of pure water at 32° F and the boiling point of water at 212° F (at sea level).
- The temperature is usually reported in degrees Fahrenheit in newspapers, on the radio, and on television.
- The normal mouth temperature of the human body is 98.6° F on this scale.

Celsius

- The Celsius thermometer records temperatures based on the freezing point of pure water at 0° C and a boiling point of water at 100° C (at sea level).
- The Celsius thermometer is used in most countries other than the United States because it is part a of a metric system.
- The Celsius thermometer is usually used by scientists because it is based on a decimal system using multiples of ten.
- The normal mouth temperature of the human body is 37° C on this scale.

Conversion Formulas

- To convert from a Celsius temperature reading to a Fahrenheit reading, multiply the Celsius reading by 9, divide that product by 5, and add 32.

   (°C x 9) ÷ 5 + 32 = ° F

- To convert from a Fahrenheit reading to a Celsius reading, first subtract 32 from the Fahrenheit reading, then multiply the difference by 5 and divide the product by 9.

   (°F − 32) x 5 ÷ 9 = ° C

Here are the two thermometers:

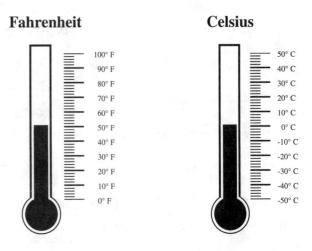

A Fahrenheit thermometer has a reading of 50° F. How much is this above the freezing point of water and below the boiling point of water?

Subtract 32 from 50. (50 − 32 = 18)

The answer is 18 degrees above the freezing point of water.

Subtract 50 from 212. (212 − 50 = 162)

The answer is 162 degrees below the boiling point of water.

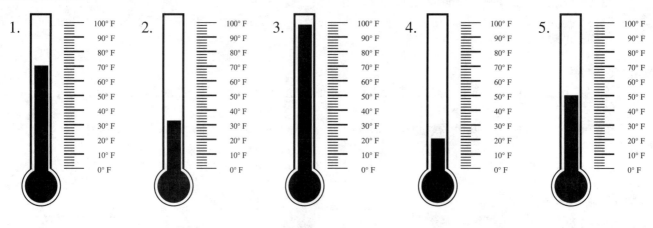

Directions: Record the readings on these Fahrenheit thermometers on the line beneath to each thermometer.

Directions: Use the information from page 37 to answer these questions.

6. What is the normal temperature of the human body (°F)? _____

   How much less than 99° F is a normal temperature? _____

7. What temperature is 20 degrees above the freezing point of water? _____

8. How many degrees below the freezing point of water is 0° F? _____

9. How many degrees Fahrenheit separate the freezing point of water from the boiling point of water? _____

10. How many degrees below the boiling point of water is the normal temperature of the human body (°F)? _____

11. If a person has a fever-induced temperature of 103° F, how much higher than normal is that temperature? _____

12. How far below the freezing point of water is a temperature of 40° below zero? _____

13. Arizona had a record high air temperature of 128° F in 1994. How much higher than the normal human body temperature was this? _____

14. Alaska recorded a temperature of –80° F (eighty degrees below zero). How much lower than the freezing point of water is this record? _____

Directions: Record the readings on these Celsius thermometers on the line below each thermometer.

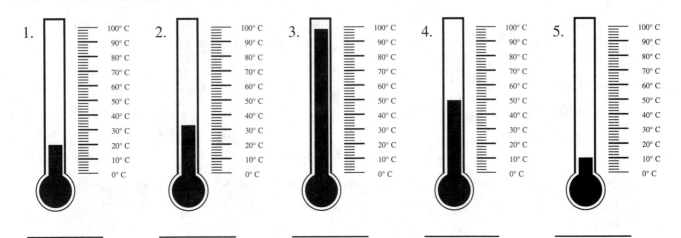

Directions: Use the information from page 37 to answer these questions.

6. What is a normal room temperature (68°F) in degrees Celsius? _____

7. Would a temperature of 50° C be uncomfortably cold, uncomfortably hot,
   or about right? _____

8. What is the freezing point of water in degrees Celsius? _____

9. How much hotter than boiling water is 122° C? _____

10. How much lower than the freezing point of water is a temperature of –40° C? _____

11. What reading is exactly half way between boiling water and the point where
    water freezes? _____

12. The lowest Antarctica reading was –89° C. How many degrees below
    freezing was this? _____

Directions: Match the clothing in the second column with the appropriate Celsius reading in the first column.

Column I

_____ 13. 20° C

_____ 14. 35° C

_____ 15. -5° C

_____ 16. 15° C

_____ 17. -30° C

Column II

A. heavy parka

B. ice skates

C. short sleeves

D. light jacket

E. swim suit

The formula for converting Celsius temperatures to the Fahrenheit scale is (C x 9) ÷ 5 + 32 = °F. **Sample: Convert 20°C to °F** **(20 x 9) ÷ 5 + 32 = 68° F** **20°C = 68° F**	The formula for converting Fahrenheit temperatures to the Celsius scale is (F – 32) x 5 ÷ 9 = °C. **Sample: Convert 50°F to °C** **(50 – 32) x 5 ÷ 9 = 10° F** **50°F = 10° C**

Directions: Use the information above to convert each of these Fahrenheit readings to the Celsius scale. Round answers to the nearest degree. Compare the Celsius and the Fahrenheit thermometers at the bottom of the page to check your answers.

1. 40° F = _____ ° C

2. 68° F = _____ ° C

3. 100° F = _____ ° C

4. 80° F = _____ ° C

5. 32° F = _____ ° C

6. 212° F = _____ ° C

Directions: Use the information above to convert each of these Celsius readings to the Fahrenheit scale. Round answers to the nearest degree. Compare the Celsius and the Fahrenheit thermometers at the bottom of the page to check your answers.

7. 25° C = _____ ° F

8. 10° C = _____ ° F

9. 37° C = _____ ° F

10. 75° C = _____ ° F

11. 30° C = _____ ° F

12. 60° C = _____ ° F

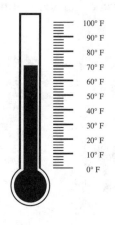

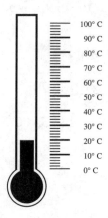

The formula for determining the rate of speed follows:

rate of speed = distance divided by time or r = $\frac{d}{t}$

Example: If a car travels 120 miles in 3 hours, what is its average speed in miles per hour?

r = 120/3

r = 40 miles per hour

The formula for determining the distance traveled follows:

distance = rate of speed multiplied by the time or d = r x t

Example: If a car traveled 40 miles per hour for 3 hours, how far did it travel?

d = 40 x 3

d = 120 miles

Directions: Use the information above to solve these problems.

1. Your best friend rode his bike 45 miles in 5 hours. What was your friend's average rate of speed? _____ miles per hour

2. You rode your skateboard across town at 15 miles per hour for 3 hours. How far did you ride? _____ miles

3. A fifth grade teacher drove 450 miles from Los Angeles to Sacramento in 9 hours. What was her average rate of speed? _____ m.p.h.

4. Your principal drove 2,800 miles from New York City to Seattle, Washington, in 64 hours. What was his or her average rate of speed? _____ m.p.h.

5. A group of Eagle Scouts traveled the 2,800 miles from New York City to Seattle by bicycle in 250 hours. What was their average rate of speed? _____ m.p.h.

6. A troop of Girl Scouts bicycled at 14 miles per hour for 12 hours. How many miles did they travel? _____ miles

7. A man rode a horse at 18 miles per hour for 15 hours. How far did he travel? _____ miles

8. An airplane flew 3,471 miles from New York City to London, England, in 6 hours. What was the average rate of speed? _____ m.p.h.

9. Charles Lindbergh flew 3,610 miles nonstop from New York to Paris in $33\frac{1}{2}$ hours. What was his average speed in miles per hour? _____ m.p.h. (Round your answer to the nearest tenth.)

10. Amelia Earhart flew about 2,025 miles from Newfoundland, Canada, to Ireland in about 15 hours. What was her average rate of speed? _____ m.p.h.

If you know the distance an object traveled and its rate of speed, you can compute the time it took to travel that distance.

time = distance divided by rate of speed or $t = \dfrac{d}{r}$

Example: A car traveled 100 miles at 50 miles per hour. How long did it take the car to travel that distance?

$$t = \frac{d}{r} = \frac{100}{50} = 2 \text{ hours}$$

Directions: Use the information from page 41 and the model above to help you compute these answers.

1. A member of a bicycle club rode his bicycle 100 miles at 10 miles per hour. How many hours did he ride? _____ hr.

2. A pilot flew her 1930s era single engine plane 450 miles at 150 miles per hour. How many hours did she fly? _____ hr.

3. Your mother drove 100 miles at 40 miles per hour. How many hours did she drive? _____ hr.

4. You rode your new skates a total distance of 35 miles in 5 hours. What was your rate of speed? _____ m.p.h.

5. You and your best friend rode your bicycles on a 75-mile camping trip at an average speed of 10 miles per hour. How many hours did you ride? _____ hr.

6. A sixth grade teacher at Olsen Elementary School drove 3,095 miles from Boston, Massachusetts, to San Francisco, California, in 59 hours. What was her rate of speed? (Round the answer to the nearest tenth.) _____ m.p.h.

7. Two athletes decided to walk 3,150 miles from Los Angeles to New York. Their walking speed was 4 miles per hour. How many hours did it take them? _____ hr.

8. Two college students decided to drive 1,880 miles from Atlanta to Salt Lake City in a golf cart at an average speed of 16 miles per hour. How many hours did it take them to make the trip? _____ hr.

9. A motorcyclist decided to ride his motorcycle 608 miles from Washington, D.C., to Atlanta, Georgia. His rate of speed was 45 miles per hour. How many hours did it take him? _____ hr.

10. A young pilot flew her single engine plane 1,545 miles from Los Angeles, California to Mexico City at an average speed of 103 miles per hour. How many hours did the flight take? _____ hr.

In order to solve geometric problems, some general principles are used. Axioms, at one time called "self-evident truths," are basic mathematical principles. There are several axioms with which you may already be familiar since you have probably performed mathematical operations using them. Think of a situation in which you used this axiom: "If equals are added to equals, the sums are equal."

Here is an axiom.

The whole is greater than any of its parts, and it is equal to the sum of all of its parts.

Can you demonstrate that the whole is equal to the sum of its parts using the polygons below? Cut out the polygons and arrange them so that they form a square. Then, find the necessary areas to show that this axiom is correct. To help you get started, use the following information:

- The area of section D is 12 cm².
- The area of the whole (square) is 144 cm².

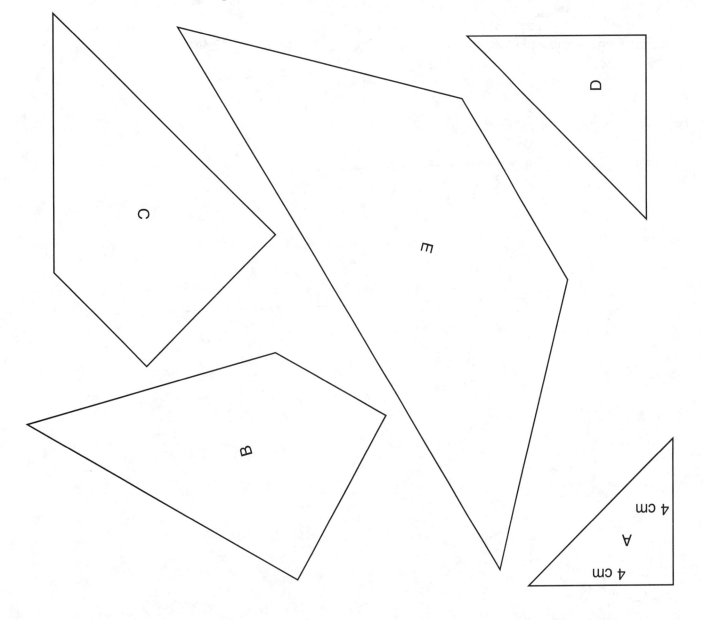

Each triangle has three angles. Angles have a vertex (point) and two sides (rays). Angles are measured by degrees. If one ray makes one whole revolution, it will sweep 360°.

A right angle measures 90°. Any angle less than a right angle is an acute angle. Any angle greater than a right angle and less than a straight angle is called an obtuse angle. Now you have four angles you can refer to: *acute, right, obtuse*, and *straight*. (The other angle which is not often used is a *reflex* angle. This is an angle that is more than 180°.)

Find and name (acute, right, obtuse, straight, or reflex) all the angles in this figure. Make a chart showing all the angles you found and label each angle with its correct name.

Types of Angles

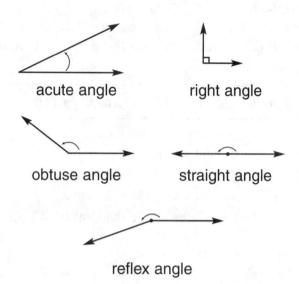

acute angle   right angle

obtuse angle   straight angle

reflex angle

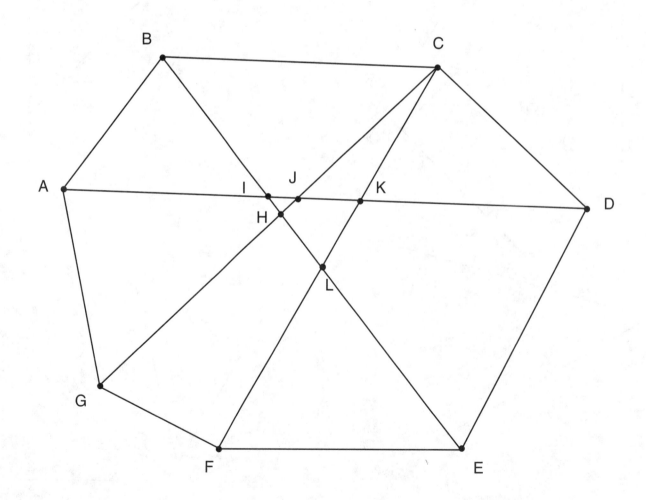

Directions: Using a computer spreadsheet program like *Microsoft Excel,* create a chart that lists the measurements in both U. S. Customary and Metric of items that you find in your home or classroom. (**Note:** The directions below are specifically written for *Microsoft Excel* but can be modified for any spreadsheet program.)

1. Before you begin work on the computer, write a list of items that you might find in your home or classroom that you want to measure the lengths and widths of. Measure and record the lengths of these items.

2. Type the word "Item" for the title of the first column. Then type "length (in.)" for the title for the second column, "length (cm)" for the third column, "width (in.)" for the title for the fourth column, and "width (cm)" for the title for the last column. You may have to widen the width of the columns by clicking your mouse on the margin of each column and moving it to the right.

3. Enter the information for the first two columns (item and length (in.)) and then for the third column (length (cm)), enter the formula "= SUM(B2*2.54)" in cell C2 and then highlight the rest of the column and go to the **Edit Toolbar** and select **FILL**. Then select **Down** for the direction in which you want your column filled with the same formula that was placed in cell C2.

4. Enter the information for the fourth column (width (in.)); and then for the fifth column (width (cm)), enter the formula "=SUM(D2*2.54)" in cell E2. Next, highlight the rest of the column E and go to the **Edit Toolbar** and select **FILL**. Then select **Down** for the direction in which you want your column filled with the same formula that was placed in cell E2.

5. You can add a title to your chart by typing a header to your *Excel* file.

6. Save and print your chart.

Samples

Item	Length (in.)	Length (cm)	Width (in.)	Width (cm)
book	5	12.7	7	17.78
bed	84	213.36	48	121.92
desk	60	152.4	48	121.92
lamp	15	38.1	12	30.48
bookshelf	48	121.92	30	76.2
stereo	12	30.48	18	45.72

Measurements of Things in My Room

Item	Length (in.)	Length (cm)	Width (in.)	Width (cm)
book	5	12.7	7	17.78
bed	84	213.36	48	121.92
desk	60	152.4	48	121.92
lamp	15	38.1	12	30.48
bookshelf	48	121.92	30	76.2
stereo	12	30.48	18	45.72

This chart shows the size of 10 states by land area measured in square miles.

State	Area (Square Miles)	Rank
Alabama	52,423 sq. mi.	30th
Alaska	656,424 sq. mi.	1st
California	163,707 sq. mi.	3rd
Delaware	2,489 sq. mi.	49th
Florida	65,756 sq. mi.	22nd
Hawaii	10,932 sq. mi.	43rd
Indiana	36,420 sq. mi.	38th
Massachusetts	10,555 sq. mi.	44th
Rhode Island	1,545 sq. mi.	50th
Texas	268,601 sq. mi.	2nd

Use this Internet address, an almanac, or an encyclopedia to find information about other states.

http://www.50states.com/

1. How many square miles larger is the 49th largest state than the 50th largest state? _____

2. How much larger is Alaska than Texas? _____

3. What is the difference in area between the largest and smallest state?_____

4. Which state is the 25th greatest in size? _____

5. Which state is the 4th greatest in size? _____

Use this Internet address to help you find the information needed to answer these questions.

http://www.un.org/Pubs/CyberSchoolBus/infonation/e_i_map.htm

6. Find the number of square kilometers in your state (or nation). Find the number of square kilometers in five other nations in the world. (Most other nations use square kilometers instead of miles.)

	1	2	3	4	5	6
Name						
Area (Square Kilometers)						

7. Which of the nations you chose has the fewest people per square kilometer?_____

Page 6
1. 5 11/16"
2. 2 5/16"
3. 6 3/4"
4. 6 7/16"
5.–18. Answers will vary.

Pages 7 and 8
Answers will vary.

Page 10
1. 18.2 cm
2. 26.2 cm
3. 13½ cm
4. 16½ ft.
5. 15¼ in.
6. 18⅜ cm.
7.–10. Answers will vary.

Page 11
1. 15.6 cm
2. 11¼ in.
3. 24.4 m
4. 18¾ ft.
5. 74.4 m
6. 64 yd.
7. 137.4 cm
8. 105.3 m

Page 12
1. 19.1 m
2. 22.6 m
3. 26 in.
4. 20½ ft.
5. 25.12 m
6. 37.68 in.
7. 31.4 cm
8. 21.98 m

Page 14
1. 41 m²
2. 126 yd.²
3. 67.5 cm²
4. 6.08 m²
5. 34 ft.²
6. 16 1/4 in.²
7. 3,680 m²
8. 7,500 mm²

Page 15
1. 24 ft.²
2. 45 yd.²
3. 11.66 cm²
4. 27.72 cm²

5. 405 in.²
6. 49.14 m²
7. 116.39 cm²
8. 86.45 m²

Page 16
1. 50.24 m²
2. 78.5 cm²
3. 314 cm²
4. 452.16 cm²
5. 1,256 cm²
6. 615.44 ft.²
7. 706.5 in.²
8. 1,962.5 m²

Page 18
1. 105 m³
2. 720 ft.³
3. 343 cm³
4. 165 in.³
5. 240 yd.³
6. 67.032 m³
7. 92.736 m³
8. 694.512 cm³
9. 1,728 ft.³
10. 86 6/8 ft.³

Page 19
1. 351.68 m³
2. 169.56 cm³
3. 282.6 cm³
4. 18.84 in.³
5. 50,240 cm³
6. 1,538.6 ft.³

Pages 20–23
Answers will vary.

Page 24
1. 6 lbs. 4 oz.
2. 1 ton 300 lbs.
3. 4,000 cassettes
4. 100 pills
5. 100,000 pills
6. 2,000 dictionaries
7. 12,000 staplers
8. 100 people
9. 500 mg or 1/2 g
10. 220 kg
11. 4,400 kg
12. 2,200 clips
13. 6,400 calculators
14. 40 cameras

Page 26
1. 8 fl. oz.
2. 16 fl. oz.
3. 32 fl. oz.
4. 48 fl. oz.
5. 64 fl. oz.
6. 72 fl. oz.
7. 32 fl. oz.
8. 64 fl. oz.
9. 160 fl. oz.
10. 96 fl. oz.
11. 4 qt.
12. 16 qt.
13. 128 fl. oz.
14. 60 qt.
15. 1,920 fl. oz.
16. 16 fl. oz.
17. 48 fl. oz.
18. 112 fl. oz.
19. 40 pints
20. 176 cups
21. 120 pints
22. 1,280 fl. oz.
23. 34 cups
24. 176 fl. oz.
25. 344 fl. oz.

Page 27
1. 30 mL
2. 240 mL
3. 1,000 mL
4. 960 mL
5. 40 mL
6. 480 mL
7. 3,840 mL
8. 3.84 L
9. 38.4 L
10. 69.1 L
11. 960 L
12. 96 L
13. 96 L
14. 1920
15. 360 L

Page 28
1. 2 qt.
2. 12 mL
3. 80 mL
4. 336 mL
5. 50 pennies
6. 432 mL

7. 24 fl. oz.
8. 384 mL
9. 128 quarters
10. 19.2 L
11. 8 times
12. 48 cups

Page 30
1. 40° acute
2. 120° obtuse
3. 180° straight
4. 90° right
5. 50° acute
6. 130° obtuse
7. 250° reflex
8. 215° reflex
9. 90° right
10. 80° acute

Page 31
1. <BAC = 100°
   <CBA = 35°
   <ACB = 45°
   △ABC = 180°
2. <CDE = 50°
   <ECD = 70°
   <DEC = 60°
   △DEC = 180°
3. <LMN = 90°
   <MNL = 30°
   <MLN = 60°
   △LMN = 180°
4. <MNO = 25°
   <OMN = 65°
   <MON = 90°
   △MNO = 180°
5. <XYZ = 60°
   <ZXY = 60°
   <YZX = 60°
   △XYZ = 180°
6. <WPO = 154°
   <POW = 11°
   <PWO = 15°
   △WPO = 180°

Page 32

Page 34

1. 3 hr 35 min
2. 1 hr 40 min
3. 6 hr 25 min
4. 6 hr 55 min
5. 2 hr 35 min
6. 8 hr 6 min
7. 7 hr 56 min
8. 2 hr 16 min
9. 190 days 13 hr 32 min
10. 91 days 3 hr 39 min
11. 34 wk 3 days 14 hr 40 min
12. 15 wk 6 days 5 hr 6 min
13. 26 days 12 hr 34 min
14. 13 days 19 hr 25 min

Page 35

1. Feb./Mar.
2. Ending in 29, the first month must be February.
3. Feb. 19th
4. Apr. 4th
5. Mar. 18th
6. 5
7. 31 days
8. 275 days
9. Mar. 1
10. December 26th
11. April 23rd
12. Monday

Page 36

(dates as of year 2000)

1. 378 yr.
2. 3,800 yr.
3. 369 yr.
4. 187 yr.
5. 3,000 yr.
6. 2,100 yr.
7. 383 yr.
8. 334 yr.

Page 38

1. 70° F
2. 32° F
3. 98° F
4. 20° F
5. 50° F
6. 98.6° F; .4° F
7. 52° F
8. 32° F
9. 180° F
10. 113.4° F
11. 4.4° F
12. 72° F
13. 29.4° F
14. 112° F

Page 39

1. 20° C
2. 33° C
3. 98° C
4. 50° C
5. 10° C
6. 20° C
7. 122° F uncomfortably hot
8. 0° C
9. 22° C
10. 40° C
11. 50° C
12. 89° C
13. C. short sleeves
14. E. swim suit
15. B. ice skates
16. D. light jacket
17. A. heavy parka

Page 40

1. 4° C
2. 20° C
3. 38° C
4. 27° C
5. 0° C
6. 100° C
7. 77° F
8. 50° F
9. 99° F (98.6° F)
10. 167° F
11. 86° F
12. 140° F

Page 41

1. 9 m.p.h.
2. 45 miles
3. 50 m.p.h.
4. 43.75 m.p.h.
5. 11.2 m.p.h.
6. 168 miles
7. 270 miles
8. 578.5 m.p.h.
9. 107.8 m.p.h.
10. 135 m.p.h.

Page 42

1. 10 hr.
2. 3 hr.
3. 2.5 hr.
4. 7 m.p.h.
5. 7.5 hr.
6. 52.5 m.p.h.
7. 787.5 hr.
8. 117.5 hr.
9. 13.5 hr.
10. 15 hr.

Page 43

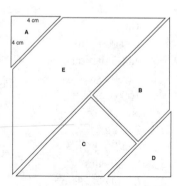

Area of square = 144 cm²
Area of parts (A + B + C + D + E) = 144 cm²
Possible steps to finding the areas of each part:
To find the area of section E (64 cm²), subtract the area of A (8 cm²) from the area of one-half the square (72 cm²).
Section B and section C are congruent. Sections B, C, and D make up one-half the square. To find the area of B (30), subtract the area of D (12 cm²) from the areas of B + C + D (72 cm²), and then divide that difference by 2.
Section areas in square centimeters: A = 8, B = 30, C = 30, D = 12, E = 64
The sum of the parts (8 + 30 + 30 + 12 + 64) = the whole (144).

Pages 44 and 45

Answers will vary.

Page 46

1. 944 mi.²
2. 387,823 mi.²
3. 654,879 mi.²
4. Illinois
5. Montana
6.–7. Answers will vary.